PHOTOGRAPHS
Larry Prosor

WORDS
Richard Moreno

CAPTIONS
Larry Prosor

DESIGN
Dean Eichler
Larry Prosor

PRODUCTION
Larry Prosor
David Zischke
Sean Van Dyne

EDITED
Laurel Hilde

NEVADA

Desert Lows & Mountain Highs

A PHOTO ESSAY BY LARRY PROSOR

A special thanks to the following people who helped make this book possible.

Greg Cichoski
Jim King
Robert Laxalt
Laurel Hilde Lippert
Silver and Bill Martin
Nicole Misfeldt
Nevada Commission on Tourism
Nevada Magazine
Nadine Powers
Cindy, Whitney and Will Prosor
The Prunty Family
R & R Advertising
Ruby Mountain Heli Ski
Skydance Helicopters
Rob Stillwell
"The Professional Tourists"
Tom Radco and the staff at University of Nevada Press
Jerry Vaughn
Nancy Nell Vaughn

Limited edition, high quality photographic prints from this book can be obtained through:

Larry Prosor Photography
P.O. Box 2375
Truckee, CA 96161
916-587-4736

Additional books, calendars, posters and cards can be ordered through:

Fine Line Productions
P.O. Box 2452
Truckee, CA 96160
916-587-0760

CONTENTS

*T*HE SUNSET MEANS RELIEF

TO MANY ANIMALS THAT TAKE

SHELTER FROM THE GLARING

SUN UNDERGROUND, IN THE

SHADE, OR IN AN AIR-CONDI-

TIONED BUILDING.

FOREWORD

Robert Laxalt

As I looked at Larry Prosor's photographs and read Rich Moreno's prose, one thought kept running through my mind: what this book is saying is like a biblical simile. In the beginning was the land and in the end there will remain only the land.

The reader will know what I mean as he explores this book. Neither image nor prose stray far from the land. Geologic ages of volcanic eruption, searing sun and glacial cold come and go. Primitive man appears, lays his imprint gently with haunting petroglyphs and then fades into the mystery of oblivion. The white man comes and confronts the wilderness of desert and mountain as an enemy to be conquered. Emigrant trains and fortune-seeking successors tear pell-mell across the forbidding desert sweeps with one thought in mind—to reach the green promised land of California as quickly as they can. The gold seekers curse the obstacles and the hardships of the land, their eyes only upon the treasure-bearing rivers and streams of the Sierra. They come reluctantly back to the desolation of Nevada when silver makes any setting desirable, and then leave when they have plundered the land. They build myriad little mining camps and towns that live for a day or a handful of years before they begin to crumble into the enduring land that has been waiting to claim them.

Only the hardy remain—cattlemen and sheepmen and town dwellers seeking a new beginning.

Photographer Larry Prosor and author Rich Moreno have probed nearly every nook and cranny of Nevada to find and chronicle the lives and visages of Nevadans gone and Nevadans present. They find beauty not in violent landscape but in hues so subtle that they seem not to exist.

They find man's presence in ways that reveal how very temporal it is. They miss practically nothing in telling the story of Nevada. And when the story is done, they conclude that when humanity has had its day in the sun, the land will be waiting still.

*C*LEAR SKIES AND THE LACK

OF CITY LIGHTS MAKE FOR IDEAL

STARGAZING.

PREFACE

Larry Prosor

In ten years of travel throughout Nevada, I have explored its deserts, mountains, cities, and small towns and have met the independent, resilient people who live here. Even with the diversity of livelihood—from rancher to casino owner, from small business owner to government worker—I've found most share a genuine pride in the state and a passion for wide-open spaces.

This vast expanse can be a harsh environment with extremes in temperature and terrrain. But, throughout Nevada, I have seen some of nature's finest work. Some of these wonders are breathtaking, while others simply make me feel at peace with the world.

Some of these oases for the soul and eyes are not always visible to those passing over Nevada at 35,000 feet or driving through on an interstate at 65 miles per hour. Perhaps that is why Nevada is perceived by some as a wasteland to be exploited as a digging and dumping ground.

It is my hope that this book will show that Nevada is a serene, sometimes primitive land with precious natural settings that should be preserved for the enjoyment of our children and their children.

Nevada is one of my favorite places. Let's hope that we learn to manage this unique environment so that future generations will be able to enjoy it as I have.

$\mathcal{T}$HE RUBY MOUNTAINS

GLOW IN THE DAY'S LAST RAYS

OF SUNSHINE.

THE STATE

"The Pearl of the West" - Horace Greeley

Nevada is a trapezoid-shaped piece of the American West, bordered by the states of California, Oregon, Idaho, Utah, and Arizona. The seventh largest state, it encompasses 110,540 square miles and is 485 miles long, 315 miles wide.

While it has more than 200 mountain ranges, it is the driest state. Altitudes range from over 13,000 feet to less than 1,000 feet. Average annual daily temperatures range from 70 degrees Fahrenheit in the south to 45 degrees in the north.

Nevada is a vast area of north-south mountain ranges separated by wide, parallel valleys. The mountains are largely vegetated by juniper and piñon pine forests, while the long valleys are covered with sagebrush, grease-wood, various grasses, and, in the south, mesquite, yucca, and Joshua trees.

Due to the harsh, difficult conditions, Nevada's earliest residents were a nomadic people subsisting on the available scarce resources, including fish, rabbits, insects, nuts, roots, grasses, and the limited wildlife.

Then, the "Taibo," or white man, came.

$\mathcal{L}$AYERS OF GEOLOGIC TIME

ARE REVEALED AT RED ROCKS.

OVERVIEW

"Hidden between the pages was a single sprig of Nevada sagebrush.
Before I could protect myself, the memories were summoned up
and washed over me in a flood."

Robert Laxalt

For more than a century and a quarter, Nevada has charmed, disturbed, perplexed and, to borrow a word from former Nevadan Mark Twain, "bamboozled" those who would try to fit it into some neat definition. It is a place that has been described as both a "vacant sunburnt space between the gambling ghettos and the Mormon Tabernacle Choir" as well as a "beautiful desert of buried hopes."

To the early explorers, it was "the great unknown" and a place to be avoided, while in recent years it has been looked upon as a wasteland suitable only for the nation's nuclear waste. With its miles of open, untamed, seemingly vacant landscape, it's easy to understand why, at first, some might not recognize the unique beauty found in Nevada.

But Nevada has a way of changing a person. What once may have looked like a big, empty desert valley, in time, becomes a complex, thriving community of sagebrush, greasewood, piñon, rice grass, and dozens of other plants, animals, and insects. What once may have seemed merely a lonely evening sky transforms into a visual feast of rich, purple-red hues, later accented by a bright moon that casts a luminous glow on the desert. What once appeared to be some remote, probably boring, backwater town turns out to be a hidden treasure-trove of fascinating characters, history and scenery.

There are plenty of reasons why Nevada is the way it is. Over the past half-billion years, the land area now called Nevada has been submerged under a sea, dried out under an unbearably hot sun, plunged back under water, lifted out, squeezed, folded, sand-blasted, cooked by lava, buried under volcanic ash, covered with ice and more water, before finally drying

out and becoming what it is today—you'll have to agree that it's tough to maintain a sunny disposition after all that.

Modern Nevada began to take shape about 15 million years ago, during the last of the seemingly endless upheavals that assaulted the state. During this era, called the Miocene epoch, the continental plates under the land began to shift, lifting the crust upward. This action caused the surface to pull apart, then slide together, ultimately creating the 200-plus mountain ridges in the state as well as the many magnificent, wide valleys. Later, some 10 million years ago, the Sierra Nevada, the western border of the region, underwent one final uplifting, which, this time, placed everything east of the range in its shadow, changing weather patterns and creating the desert climate to the east.

One of the first non-native visitors to the region, John C. Frémont, erroneously named it the "Great Basin" upon seeing that its rivers drained into lakes or evaporated into sinks and did not flow to an ocean like most other rivers. The reality, however, is that rather than being a giant bowl ringed by mountains, Nevada's surface is a washboard of hundreds of ridges and depressions, nearly all running north to south—but the "Great Washboard" doesn't quite have the same ring as the "Great Basin." The hundreds of Nevada mountain ranges generally run 50 to 100 miles in length and are separated by valleys of about equal length.

Archaeological evidence indicates the presence of people in the region about 12,000 years ago, just as the great lakes covering the state were beginning to recede. Additionally, prehistoric rock writings, called petroglyphs, have been found at nearly 100 sites throughout the state. While the exact meaning of these stone designs has never been determined, petroglyphs have been found dating back more than 5,000 years.

A more sophisticated Indian culture began to develop in southern Nevada after 2,500 B.C. Initially foragers who traveled in small bands, these early emigrants (who most likely spread into Nevada from the southwest) subsisted on such delicacies as desert tortoise, jack rabbits, and screwbeans.

About 300 B.C., the Anasazi appeared on the Nevada scene, bringing more evolved skills such as basket making and the ability to construct pit houses, which were holes dug in the ground with roofs made of brush and grass. Within a few hundred years, the Anasazi began developing communities in which many members of the tribe lived in close proximity to each other, hunted and gathered together and built homes of adobe.

The Anasazi disappeared about 1150, perhaps as the result of a severe drought or epidemic. This coincided with the emergence of the Southern Paiute culture (who lived in southern and southeastern Nevada), as well as the related Western Shoshones (eastern, central and northeastern Nevada) and Northern Paiutes (northwest and western Nevada). A fourth group, the Washo, roamed parts of western Nevada and eastern California (Honey Lake to Sonora Pass to the Virginia City area). With a language and culture different from those of its Nevada neighbors, the Washo tribe was more closely related to the Miwok Indians of eastern California.

Not surprisingly, the environment dictated the lifestyles of Nevada's tribes. Since survival depended on following seasonal harvests, fishing and hunting, Nevada's native people did not construct permanent homes or develop sophisticated agriculture. Dwellings consisted largely of temporary structures made of poles covered with reeds, branches and grass. The exception was in winter when tribes would relocate to more sheltered valleys and construct grass or bark dwellings.

Early Explorations

While Nevada's native people were able to maintain a tenuous balance with their environment

in order to survive, the arrival of the white man ("Taibo" in the Paiute language) ultimately presented a far greater threat to their continued existence.

The first visitor is believed to be Father Francisco Garcés, although there is disagreement about whether he traveled far enough north to cross the boundaries of the modern state. In the spring of 1776, Garcés and two Indian guides split off from a larger expedition force led by Captain Juan Bautista de Anza to seek a more direct route from Santa Fe to Monterey (the famed "Old Spanish Trail"). Garcés crossed the Colorado River near the southern tip of the state.

The first major non-Indian penetrations into the region occurred in 1826 when Jedediah Smith and Peter Skene Ogden, representing rival fur trading companies, led two expeditions into the area, each from opposite directions. Both explorers were also searching for the mythical San Buenaventura River, a waterway that was believed to drain western rivers into the Pacific Ocean.

Smith, who represented the American-owned Rocky Mountain Fur Company, led his party through southern Nevada, spent the winter in California, then returned in the spring over the Sierra Nevada range, before surviving a trek across central Nevada. The group's trip was significant because it was the first to cross the wide expanse of the Great Basin as well as question the existence of the San Buenaventura River.

That same year, Ogden, who worked for the British-owned Hudson's Bay Company, led a party into the future Silver State from the north, trapping beaver along the Humboldt River. In the fall of 1828, he set out from Oregon, entering Nevada near present-day Denio, and continued south until he encountered a river (the Humboldt, which he named "Unknown River").

His group headed east to Salt Lake City due to the coming winter months, passing near the future site of Elko. The following spring, Ogden returned to Nevada in search of more beaver pelts and explored much of northeastern Nevada before heading west along the Humboldt River, eventually reaching the Humboldt Sink. In 1829, Ogden again returned to Nevada, this time retracing his trail along the Humboldt River to the Humboldt Sink, then heading south to present Walker Lake, before turning south into California. He found no proof of an inland river leading to the Pacific Ocean.

The next forays into the region occurred in the early 1830s with the explorations of the Captain Joseph Walker party, which retraced Odgen's route to the Humboldt Sink before crossing the Sierra near present Bridgeport. On the return trip, Walker's group crossed into Nevada farther south and traveled north to the Humboldt Sink. After following the Humboldt River as far east as Wells, the party ventured northeast, establishing a route that became part of the California Trail.

The Early Emigrants

Word of these early successful crossings of the region and excitement over the economic opportunities to be found in California ignited the imaginations of a number of individuals, including Missouri schoolteacher John Bidwell, who formed the Western Emigration Society.

In 1841, Bidwell, along with John Bartleson and other families eager for new opportunities, set out for California. The large group arrived at Soda Springs on Idaho's Bear River, then split into several smaller parties, each choosing a different route. The bulk of the emigrants headed south on the more familiar Santa Fe Trail, while the Bidwell-Bartleson group struck out southwest into the Great Salt Flats and Nevada. While making many mistakes during the journey, and barely surviving, the party managed to arrive in California about six months after departing Missouri and established the overland travel to the West. A second group, the Walker-Chiles party, traveled a slightly different route in 1843, largely avoiding the salt flats, and arrived in California nearly intact.

Large-scale migration to the west followed the highly publicized explorations of Captain John C. Fré-

mont. From 1843 to 1853, Frémont led a team of explorers, including Kit Carson, which made several trips into northern, central and southern Nevada, mapping much of the state and providing lasting names to many landmarks, ranging from Pyramid Lake to the Humboldt River.

Frémont's widely circulated report to Congress, following his 1843-44 and 1845 journeys, included the first accurate maps of the region and provided the tangible proof—which was heavily biased by Frémont's firm belief in Manifest Destiny and his desire to settle the West—that many needed before attempting the treacherous journey to California. Starting in 1846, with the ill-fated Donner Party, hundreds of caravans of wagons, horses and people began heading west.

The Donner Party was a group of emigrants that had departed Independence, Missouri, for California on May 5, 1846. Originally part of a larger group, the Donner Party, which included 87 men, women and children, split off on their own to follow a "shortcut" called the Hastings Cutoff. Unfortunately, the cutoff did not exist and only served to delay the group.

The party finally reached the Truckee Meadows area (future site of Reno) in October. After resting, the group attempted to cross the Sierra Nevada range just at the onset of one of the worst winters in history. A nearly continuous series of heavy snowstorms and blizzards trapped the travelers near the shores of Donner Lake where they were forced to spend weeks without supplies. By the time relief parties finally arrived from California, forty of the original party had perished.

The Gold Seekers

Despite the Donner legacy, the discovery of gold in California in January 1848 finally opened wide the

*A*N ABANDONED WAGON REMAINS AS WITNESS TO THE EARLY PIONEERS WHO STRUGGLED ACROSS THE VAST DESERT.

floodgates. Within months, thousands of emigrants were crossing Nevada to reach the California gold fields. Naturally, all these people required services and, within a short time, a series of trading posts and stations began appearing in Nevada.

The first significant Nevada post was established in 1850 near the eastern edge of the Sierra. This first post, really little more than a crude log cabin, was erected by Captain Joseph DeMont and Hampton S. Beatie. The two later sold their business to a man named Moore who, in turn, sold the cabin post to John Reese, a Mormon trader from Salt Lake City. Moore built a larger log structure, which became known as the Mormon Station. This building has been recognized as the first permanent structure in the first permanent settlement in the future state of Nevada.

At the same time as a small community was developing in Genoa, California-bound miners were finding specks of gold in the mountains east of the Truckee Meadows. By 1850, several dozen prospectors were working the area that became known as Gold Canyon, in the shadow of Sun Mountain. Small-scale mining operations continued in the region until 1859 with the discovery of the fabulous Comstock Lode.

While two brothers, Ethan Allan and Hosea Grosh, were the first to recognize the area's silver potential in the Gold Canyon area in 1857, it is generally recognized that the massive silver reserves of the Comstock Lode weren't uncovered until two years later by Patrick McLaughlin and Peter O'Riley.

As with many of those who were first with a major mining claim, McLaughlin and O'Riley didn't benefit much either financially or psychically from their discovery. Another miner, Henry Comstock, said he had an earlier right to the claim—most likely a lie—and gained a share of the McLaughlin-O'Riley find. In the end, it was his name that became indelibly linked with the area's huge mineral reserves.

News of the Comstock Lode spread gradually during the next months until, by 1860, thousands were making the "rush to Washoe," as it became known. A handful of mining camps were established near Sun Mountain, including Virginia City, Gold Hill and Silver City. By 1863, an estimated 15,000 people were residing in Virginia City.

Creating a State

During this same time, various attempts were made to establish some kind of governmental structure in Nevada. Initially, the area was part of the Utah Territory but that arrangement proved unsatisfactory because of the great distances to the territorial seat in Salt Lake City. After a failed attempt at unsanctioned home rule, the Nevada Territory was created by Congress in March 1861. President Abraham Lincoln named James Nye of New York as governor and Orion Clemens as territorial secretary. A territorial legislature was elected in August 1861 and met three times during the subsequent four years to establish the civil and criminal laws, revenue measures, state boundaries, and the other minutia of government.

In 1863, a constitutional convention was called to craft a document that would allow statehood. While a statewide election to approve the constitution was defeated in January 1864, enabling legislation creating the state was approved by Congress and the president on March 21, 1864. A second constitutional convention was held from July 4 through July 27, and another constitution was drafted. This version, which revised a controversial mining tax that had doomed the earlier model, was approved by a nearly ten to one margin on September 7, 1864.

On October 3, 1864, two copies of the constitution were sent to Washington, one via overland stage, and the other by steamship and rail. According to Nevada historian Phillip Earl, neither, however, had arrived in Washington by October 24. Since the enabling act required the president to have a copy to officially read into the record before issuing a proclamation of statehood, on October 26, statehood supporters decided to telegraph the 16,500-word document to President Lincoln—a task that required 12 hours of telegraph time at a cost of $3,426. On October 31, 1864, President Lincoln issued the proclamation and welcomed Nevada as the 36th state.

Mining

For the next 15 years, the fortunes of Nevada largely ebbed and flowed with those of the Comstock. While other mining districts would be created and newer towns would rise in other parts of the state, such as Austin, Belmont, and Hamilton, the Comstock would contribute nearly two-thirds of the state's total mining production from 1859 to 1880. It was no surprise that, after nearly all of Virginia City was destroyed by fire in 1875, followed by a sharp decline in the Comstock mines, and a subsequent statewide depression, some speculated that perhaps Nevada did not deserve statehood.

Ironically, Nevada's savior proved to be a rancher and sometime miner named Jim Butler, who, on May 19, 1900, stumbled upon one of the largest gold and silver discoveries of the 20th century at a place in central Nevada called Tonopah. A colorful legend has developed that says Butler's mule led him to the rich ledges at Tonopah (a Paiute name meaning "brush water"

*M*INING CORE SAMPLES LAY STREWN IN UNIONVILLE.

for springs found in the area). Regardless of the truth, Butler did find and file the original claims in the region and, with the help of mining lawyer Tasker Oddie (later elected governor and U.S. Senator) and science teacher Walter Gayhart, identified the mineral reserves.

Within months, thousands of miners had flocked to Tonopah to make their fortunes. Two years later, additional vast gold and silver deposits were uncovered about 25 miles south of Tonopah at a place eventually named Goldfield (and, in 1907, in Rhyolite). At nearly the same time, huge copper deposits were discovered in far eastern Nevada near the town of Ely.

While the major strikes at Tonopah and Goldfield helped pull the state out of its late 19th-century economic doldrums and, for a time, shifted political and economic power to central Nevada, both mining communities eventually became victims of the mining rollercoaster. By 1908, both would boast fine hotels, newspapers, dozens of substantial brick buildings, fine homes, churches and schools. And, less than a decade later, when the ore had largely run out, both would have experienced rapid declines that threatened their viability as communities. Indeed, of the early 20th-century mining boomtowns, only Ely, which had never developed as quickly or as extravagantly as its sister communities, would escape the next significant Nevada depression, during the 1920s and 1930s, as its copper reserves proved more long-lived (in fact, they lasted until the early 1980s).

Gambling

In 1931, Nevada Assemblyman Phil Tobin, a Winnemucca-area rancher, introduced legislation to legalize gambling in the state. While gambling had been alternately legal and illegal over the years—largely as a holdover from the wide-open mining camps—in 1913, all gambling was declared illegal (although card games, where the deal was alternated, was made an exception in 1915). Despite the statewide ban on gambling, enforcement of the laws was uneven at best. Tobin believed that much of the illegal gambling money was going out of state. He reasoned that legal games would help keep the money at home where it could be put to better use.

Tobin's bill was quickly approved by the state legislature and signed by Governor Fred Balzar on March 19, 1931. On the same day, Governor Balzar also signed into law a bill lowering divorce residency from three months to six weeks.

Nevada would never be the same.

L A N D

*P*YRAMID LAKE WAS ONCE A PART OF A VAST LAKE THAT COVERED AN ENORMOUS EXPANSE OF THE GREAT BASIN.

$\mathcal{T}$HE HIGHEST POINT IN NEVA-

DA AT 13,140 FEET, BOUNDARY

PEAK LIES ALONG THE CALIFOR-

NIA BORDER IN THE WHITE

MOUNTAINS. LEFT: AN ESSENTIAL

LANDMARK FOR THOUSANDS OF

SETTLERS MOVING WESTWARD

WAS THE "BLACK ROCK." HERE,

IN A BROAD EXPANSE OF ARID

LAND, WAS A WELCOME OASIS.

𝓜OONSET OVER THE INDE-
PENDENCE RANGE. LEFT: WATER
IN THE DESERT IS A PRECIOUS
COMMODITY. A PASSING THUN-
DERSHOWER BRINGS MUCH-NEED-
ED MOISTURE TO THE LAND.

$\mathcal{W}$ELL-ADAPTED TO ITS LIFE IN

THE DESERT, A LARGE JOSHUA

TREE REACHES OUT TO THE SET-

TING SUN. RIGHT: NOTHING

CLEANSES THE MIND QUITE LIKE A

WALK DOWN A TRAIL SUCH AS

THIS IN THOMAS CANYON.

A STEADY STREAM OF
WATER AND STEAM ARISES
FROM THE DESERT.

$\mathcal{T}$HE OLDEST LIVING THINGS ON EARTH, BRISTLECONE PINES, ARE KNOWN TO HAVE SURVIVED FOR ALMOST 5,000 YEARS. LEFT: ON A TYPICAL WEEKEND, SAND MOUN- TAIN BECOMES A FRENZIED ARENA FOR OFF-ROAD VEHICLES.

$\mathcal{T}$HE JARBIDGE MOUNTAINS IN
THEIR WINTER COAT. RIGHT:
LYING AT THE BASE OF COUGAR
PEAK, EMERALD LAKE IS A GEM
WORTH DISCOVERING.

$\mathcal{W}$ATER IS A PRECIOUS COM-

MODITY IN SOME PLACES OF NEVA-

DA BUT AN ABUNDANT RESOURCE

IN OTHERS. LEFT: THE JOSHUA

TREE STANDS TALL, EVIDENCE OF ITS

ABILITY TO STORE WATER.

*T*HOUGH NEVADA IS MOSTLY

ARID, WATERY GEMS LIKE TOPAZ

LAKE ARE SCATTERED ACROSS

THE STATE.

SHIFTING SANDS CREATE EVER-
CHANGING PATTERNS SCULPTED
BY THE WIND. RIGHT: LOOKING
DOWN ON THE CARSON VALLEY
FROM GENOA PEAK.

$\mathcal{T}$HE MOON RISES OVER YUCCA

MOUNTAIN, A PROPOSED DUMP-

ING GROUND FOR NUCLEAR

WASTE. LEFT: MOST FIRST-TIME

VISITORS TO LAKE TAHOE WILL

SURELY REMEMBER ONE THING,

THE COLOR BLUE.

A DEAD, TWISTED PINE STANDS
AS A TESTIMONIAL TO THE HARSH-
NESS OF A HIGH ALTITUDE EXIS-
TENCE. RIGHT: VALLEY OF FIRE IS A
TWISTED MAZE OF CANYONS AND
ROCK FORMATIONS. EXPLORING A
SIDE CANYON CAN LEAD TO DIS-
COVERIES AROUND EVERY CORNER.

*S*CULPTING BY NATURE IN A

SANDY COVE ON LAKE TAHOE.

*T*HE SPRING MOUNTAIN

RANGE, EMBRACING 11,918-

FOOT MOUNT CHARLESTON,

RISES LIKE AN ISLAND ABOVE A SEA

OF SAND. LEFT: THE SHADOW OF

WHEELER PEAK STRETCHES

TOWARD THE RISING MOON ON

THE FACE OF JEFF DAVIS PEAK.

$\mathcal{A}$ FISHEYE VIEW OF ASPENS AT

SPOONER SUMMIT ON MT. ROSE.

RIGHT: A CLEARING STORM HAS

LEFT BEHIND PRECIOUS SNOW ON

THE PEAKS OF MOUNT TALLAC.

*A*N ANCIENT SEA ONCE COV-
ERED MOST PARTS OF NEVADA,
INCLUDING THIS AREA NEAR
PYRAMID LAKE. LEFT: WINTER
COMES EARLY AND STAYS LONG
IN THE HIGH PEAKS OF NEVADA.

$\mathcal{N}$EVADA IS A LAND OF
GREAT EXPANSE, INCLUDING THE
SKY ABOVE.

*T*HE VIEW FROM THE TOP OF
WHEELER PEAK ENCOMPASSES A
360-DEGREE PERSPECTIVE ON A
TRULY GREAT BASIN. RIGHT: THE
RUBY MOUNTAINS ARE HOME TO
HIMALAYAN PTARMIGAN, MOUN-
TAIN GOATS, DEER, MOUNTAIN
LIONS AND WILD TROUT.

$\mathcal{T}$HE HORIZON IS A GOOD THIR-
TY MILES AWAY WITHOUT ONE
SIGN OF MAN—A REFRESHING
SIGHT IN THIS OVERCROWDED
WORLD. LEFT: A HERD OF HORSES
ON THE MOVE TO A NEW RANGE.

SHORT DAYS AND COLD
NIGHTS SIGNAL THE ARRIVAL OF
FALL AND THE INEVITABILITY OF
WINTER. RIGHT: CATHEDRAL
GORGE CONTINUES TO CHANGE
WITH THE FORCES OF EROSION.

*T*HE BLACK ROCK DESERT'S BROAD EXPANSE HAS BEEN THE SITE OF PAST LAND SPEED RECORDS.

PEOPLE

A SUNSET REWARD FOR

THOSE WILLING TO CHASE IT.

SKIING ABOVE THE LAKE ON

THE SLOPES OF HEAVENLY.

RIGHT: THE RENO BALLOON

RACES ARE A COLORFUL FEAST

FOR THE EYES.

$\mathcal{E}$XPERIENCING FREEDOM CAMP-
ING ON LIBERTY LAKE. LEFT: THE
JARBIDGE WILDERNESS IS TRULY
UNTAMED WITH VERY FEW SIGNS
OF MAN DISRUPTING THE CYCLES
OF NATURE.

$\mathscr{F}$LY-CASTING ON SPOONER

LAKE IN THE CARSON RANGE.

LEFT: THE LAST RAYS OF THE SUN

LAY DOWN A CARPET OF GOLD

ON WHICH TO SAIL HOME.

$\mathcal{F}$LOATING ON A RAFT IN LAKE
TAHOE TAKES ON A WHOLE NEW
SENSATION WHEN YOU SEE THE
BOTTOM SO FAR BELOW.

𝓜IDWINTER PITCHFORK EXERCISE. RIGHT: A BOATER'S PARADISE, LAKE MEAD IS THE LARGEST MAN-MADE LAKE IN THE WEST.

*L*OOKING VERY SMALL ATOP A
PINNACLE IN THE RUBY MOUN-
TAINS. LEFT: SAILING ALONG ON
A SEA OF ALKALI.

*P*ADDLING AMONG TUFA

FORMATIONS AT PYRAMID

LAKE. RIGHT: HIGH ABOVE

RED ROCK CANYON.

*M*OST WHO VISIT PYRAMID

LAKE BECOME ENTRANCED BY ITS

MYSTERIOUS BEAUTY.

A SUNRISE-LACED CURTAIN

OF WATER FOLLOWS AN EARLY

MORNING WATER-SKIER. RIGHT:

FLOATING ON LAKE TAHOE'S

COLD CLEAR WATER MORE THAN

1,600 FEET DEEP.

A COWBOY'S COMMUTE TO WORK. LEFT: SKI TRACKS WEAVE THE TALES OF HAPPY SKIERS.

*C*ELEBRATING THE PAST WITH
A PARADE IN RHYOLITE. LEFT:
COWBOYS FROM ACROSS THE
COUNTRY SHOW THEIR SKILLS
AT THE RENO RODEO.

A HIKE TO THE TOP OF

SAND MOUNTAIN ISN'T EASY,

BUT THE RETURN TRIP MAKES IT

ALL WORTHWHILE. RIGHT:

WHAT IS SIMPLY A ROCK CLIFF

ADMIRED BY SOME IS A CHAL-

LENGE TO OTHERS.

OF Lake Tahoe, Mark Twain once said, "So strong was the sense of floating high aloft in mid-nothingness that we called these boat excursions 'balloon voyages'."

PLACES

*A*N ISOLATED RANCH

BENEATH THE GRANITE RANGE.

*L*IVING IN LAMOILLE MEANS
BEING SURROUNDED BY TRAN-
QUILITY AND BEAUTY. LEFT: DID
THE RAINBOW FIND THE
CHURCH, THE CHURCH FIND THE
RAINBOW, OR THE PHOTOGRA-
PHER FIND THEM BOTH?

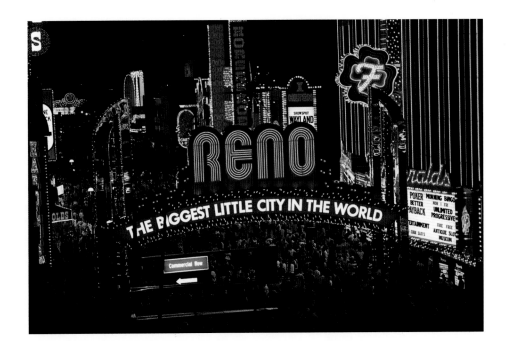

*R*ENO OWES MUCH OF ITS
EARLY DEVELOPMENT TO A MIX-
TURE OF SPEEDY DIVORCE AND
LEGALIZED GAMBLING. LEFT:
GAMBLING HAS TURNED THE
ONCE SERENE SOUTHERN SHORE
OF TAHOE INTO A HIGH-RISE
MECCA FOR LOVERS OF CHANCE.

*T*HE STATE CAPITOL IN CARSON

CITY GREW WITH THE MINING

BOOM IN NEARBY VIRGINIA CITY.

RIGHT: IN THE 1870S VIRGINIA

CITY HAD OVER ONE HUNDRED

SALOONS TO SERVE THE THIRSTY

NEEDS OF THE MINERS.

A SCENE OF QUIET LIVING IN
RURAL NEVADA.

*R*ICHES FROM THE COMSTOCK
LODE BROUGHT SUDDEN
WEALTH TO MANY VIRGINIA
CITY RESIDENTS. LEFT: THE
CARSON VALLEY WITH THE
PEAKS OF THE CARSON RANGE
SOARING ABOVE.

$\mathcal{L}$AUGHLIN, ALONG THE COL-

ORADO RIVER, IS THE LATEST

GAMING TOWN TO RISE OUT OF

THE DESERT. RIGHT: LAS VEGAS IS

A CITY PRIMARILY BUILT AROUND

THE FERVENT DESIRE OF MANY TO

PLAY AT GAMES OF CHANCE.

SOME OF THE FIRST SETTLERS

IN NEVADA CAME FOR RELIGIOUS

REASONS. A SMALL CHURCH IN

THE SMITH VALLEY BRINGS THE

COMMUNITY TOGETHER. RIGHT:

RAILROADS PLAYED A KEY ROLE

IN THE EMERGENCE OF SMALL

TOWNS ALL ACROSS THE STATE.

$\mathcal{F}$OR MANY YEARS ONE OF THE FASTEST GROWING CITIES IN AMERICA, RENO STILL HAS A QUALITY OF LIFE THAT MANY SEEK.

A FAR CRY FROM THE GLITTER-
ING "STRIP" OF LAS VEGAS.
LEFT: BUILT ALONG WITH THE
CONSTRUCTION OF HOOVER
DAM, BOULDER CITY IS THE
ONLY TOWN IN NEVADA WHERE
GAMBLING IS ILLEGAL.

$\mathcal{T}$HE EUREKA COUNTY COURT-
HOUSE STANDS FULLY RESTORED
TO ITS ORIGINAL 1879 CONDI-
TION. LEFT: THE FORMER MINING
TOWN OF JARBIDGE HAS
SHRUNK TO A HANDFUL OF PER-
MANENT RESIDENTS.

$\mathscr{B}$UILT AROUND THE MINES
OF THE COMSTOCK LODE, VIR-
GINIA CITY REMAINS A WELL-PRE-
SERVED REMINDER OF ITS COL-
ORFUL PAST. RIGHT: THE MINERS
WHO WORKED THE MINES HAD
HARSH AND OFTEN SHORT LIVES.

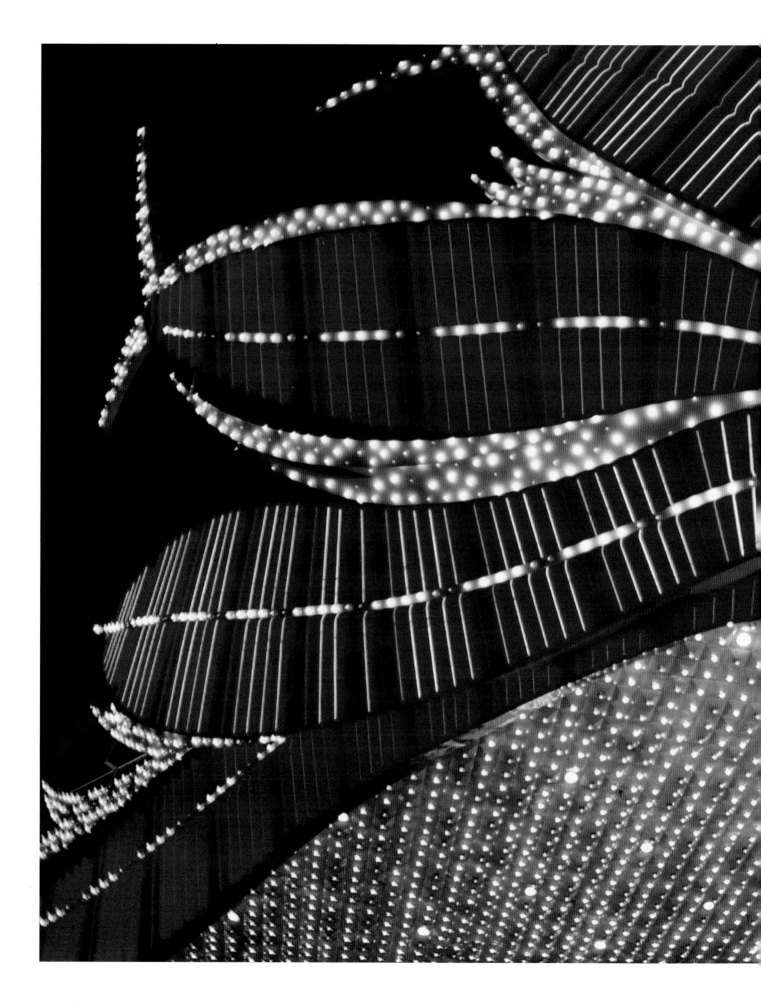

CREATING ART WITH NEON

ALONG THE VEGAS STRIP.

PAST

$\mathcal{T}$HE VAST TERRITORY WE NOW CALL NEVADA WAS ONE OF THE TOUGHEST OBSTACLES FOR THE PIONEERS WHO CROSSED IT IN COVERED WAGONS.

A NEWLY RESTORED TRAIN

FINDS A HOME IN THE RAILROAD

MUSEUM IN CARSON CITY.

LEFT: DISCARDED BOTTLES

BECOME COLLECTORS' ITEMS AS

TIME PASSES.

*G*IVING IN TO THE FORCES
OF GRAVITY IN TUSCARORA.
LEFT: MANY BURROS STILL
ROAM THE DESERTS, EVIDENCE
OF THE EARLY MINERS WHO
ABANDONED THEM.

*T*HE MIGHTY COLORADO
RIVER BACKS UP BEHIND
HOOVER DAM TO FORM LAKE
MEAD. RIGHT: THE TRAIN STA-
TION IN GOLD HILL NEAR THE
ORIGINAL DISCOVERY SITE OF THE
COMSTOCK LODE.

FRAGMENTS OF ASSORTED RANCHING TOOLS RETIRE OUTSIDE A RANCH WORKSHOP.

*E*ven a union couldn't save the jobs of its members once the gold ran dry. Left: Out of the sagebrush grew many booming mining towns. A few crumbling buildings are all that remain of the hopes and dreams of the people of Rochester.

*A*LL THAT REMAINS OF THE
RICH DIGGINGS OF GOLDFIELD
ARE THE TAILINGS LEFT BEHIND.
RIGHT: THE "BOOM AND BUST"
MINING LIFESTYLE PLAYS ON
TODAY. RUINS OF HOMES LIKE
THIS ONE IN PALMETTO ATTEST
TO A MORE LIVELY PAST.

A CRUMBLING MONUMENT TO
AN EARLY NEVADA SETTLER. RIGHT:
THE WARD CHARCOAL OVENS
WERE AT ONE TIME STACKED WITH
PIÑON PINE TO FUEL THE MARTIN
WHITE SMELTER.

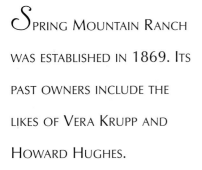

*S*PRING MOUNTAIN RANCH WAS ESTABLISHED IN 1869. ITS PAST OWNERS INCLUDE THE LIKES OF VERA KRUPP AND HOWARD HUGHES.

$\mathcal{G}$RAVEYARDS SUCH AS THIS

ONE IN VIRGINIA CITY CAN BE A

FASCINATING LOOK BACK IN HIS-

TORY. LEFT: A HOUSE BUILT OF

BOTTLES IS ONE OF THE FEW

REMAINING BUILDINGS STANDING

IN RHYOLITE TODAY.

*I*TS WALKING DAYS OVER, AN

OLD SHOE STILL HAS ITS SOLE.

LEFT: A ROADSIDE REMINDER OF

WELLINGTON'S PAST.

WHAT MEMORIES LINGER IN

AN OLD BUILDING SUCH AS

THIS. RIGHT: THE TOWERING

REMAINS OF A FORMER MILL

SITE STAND OVER THE GHOST

TOWN OF BELMONT.

*T*HE COMMUNITY CHURCH
OFTEN BROUGHT DECENCY AND
PURPOSE TO AN ISOLATED, LAW-
LESS CITIZENRY. LEFT: IN 1861
FORT CHURCHILL HOUSED OVER
FIVE HUNDRED OFFICERS AND
TROOPS WHO REGULARLY
PATROLLED THE OVERLAND
STAGE ROUTE.

A DEAD QUIET GRAVEYARD.

*I*N 1908 RHYOLITE WAS A

TOWN OF OVER 6,000 WITH

THREE RAILROADS AND FOUR

NEWSPAPERS, BUT BY 1920 IT

WAS A GHOST TOWN.

SEARCHING FOR THE WRAITHS

"And then the town died. Just died." David Toll

Scattered across the Nevada landscape are the remains of dashed hopes and busted dreams. Over the years, a trace of precious metals and the promise of untold riches have spurred more than a few folks to seek their fortunes in the Silver State.

Only a few—the Mackays, Floods, Sharons, Wingfields and a handful of others—ever made much money in mining. But that didn't discourage others from scraping away the sagebrush and chipping away at the rocks at a thousand different places in their quest for gold and silver. Time and again, a bit of color in the rocks would spark a stampede of miners, each drawn by the dream of striking it rich.

Gold Point, Goldfield, Gold Hill, Gold Center, Gold Creek, Gold Bar, Gold Acres, Gold Butte—the names might change a bit but the pattern for every mining town was essentially the same. Gold or some other precious metal would be found. Within a few months, a community would take shape in the shadow of the discovery. Merchants, saloonkeepers, whores, bankers and others would soon follow to provide the services required.

If the ore lasted more than a year, the town might take on more permanence—tent homes and businesses would be replaced by wooden storefronts and cabins. Churches would be built and a newspaper or two might be started up to proclaim to the world the vast potential of the new community.

If more than a few mining discoveries were made in the district, the town might get a few stone and, in later years, concrete buildings. A processing mill might be built to refine the ore—which at times seemed virtually limitless—being pulled from the ground.

Then, almost as quickly as it started, it would all be gone. The ore would run out. The people would begin to drift away. One by one, the buildings would be abandoned. A town would die and a ghost would be born.

In some cases, such as Virginia City and Tonopah, the town found a way to survive by embracing tourists, replacing mining with some other industry, waiting long enough for mining to come back or by just being too stubborn to die.

Perhaps because of their relative isolation, since many mining towns are tucked in remote crevices of the state, those that survive become virtual sanctuaries for those wanting to escape the structure of what passes for modern civilization. Their reasons for wanting to get away vary: they don't like crowded places, they're a little too eccentric or different; they just want to be left alone; they love the isolation. Every Nevada mining town has its own set of local characters, legends, myths and tall tales. And if you pull up a stool at almost any saloon, you might hear one or two.

Manhattan is a once prosperous central Nevada mining town that, despite its name, has disintegrated into little more than a main street of crumbling miners' shacks, a few saloons, some creaky headframes, an old wooden church and more rusted cars and abandoned equipment than is found in most wrecking yards. Outside of the town, a modern mining operation—a large open pit—reminds us of why the town exists.

There is, in Manhattan, a six-foot by six-foot piece of faded, painted plywood leaning against one of the local bars. A grid, with each square marked with a number, has been painted on one side of the wooden sheet. Three-foot-high chicken wire encloses the sides of the wooden square and the top is open.

Once, while passing through, I stopped at that

bar to use the restroom and have a soda. I asked the bartender the purpose of this unusual contraption on the side of his establishment.

"Why, that's for the chicken hit contest," he said, passing me a can of soda. "Every summer during Founders' Day, we toss a chicken in there and bet on what number he hits when he craps."

Oh.

A few years ago, a Canadian writer asked me to take him on a trip to "the real Nevada." He wanted to see a ghost town and wild horses, and he wanted to meet someone who lived in a ghost town. I said sure, and prayed for rain.

We set out from Tonopah on a cool October morning, driving east on Highway 6, then north on State Route 376, before turning northeast on the road to Belmont. We passed no traffic that day, our only companions being a handful of bleached, cotton-swab clouds floating overhead. Not much chance of rain.

The land was wide and open, so much so that the writer remarked that he was working on a book about the Trans-Canadian Highway of which this reminded him.

"Sometimes, you can see wild horses out around here," I said, eyes expectantly scanning seemingly endless miles of empty, rolling hills. "But probably not today."

Suddenly, as if on cue, a small herd of seven horses, led by a beautiful white stallion, burst from behind one of those hills and began pacing our vehicle about a quarter mile to the north.

"Do you want me to stop so you can get a picture?" I asked.

"No, they'll be gone before I could shoot it. Let's just keep driving. They're very beautiful," he said.

For another several minutes, we watched in silent admiration as those magnificent animals raced across the sagebrush. Then, as quickly as they had appeared, they veered into a hidden creek bed and were gone.

A few minutes later, we arrived at the outskirts of Belmont. We spotted a stout red brick smokestack and decided to investigate. Parking the car, we walked through the sagebrush to the ruins of the Belmont-Monitor Mill.

As we gingerly stepped around and over the scattered chunks of wood and piles of what appeared to be crushed red bricks, I heard a slapping noise overhead. I looked up into the cloudless blue sky and saw a bird passing above me. I realized the source of the strange sound. It was so peaceful you could hear the sound of a bird's wings hitting the air.

We returned to the car and resumed driving to the center of the old town of Belmont. Ahead, we could see buildings strung alongside the road and, behind them, other structures—some looking like new and others very, very old.

We stopped the car just west of the buildings and, as we climbed out, a man with a thick, gray beard, wearing a red-checked shirt with suspenders holding up a pair of baggy, gray pants appeared from a small trailer parked nearby.

"What are you doing here?" he asked. There was the strong smell of sagebrush about him—as if he'd just rolled in the stuff.

"This is a travel writer and we just wanted to do a little exploring and take a few pictures," I said.

"Well, okay, but just don't touch anything," he said, then disappeared into his trailer. We had met the man I'd heard called the Guardian of Belmont. Others had told me he watched over the premises to scare off bottle hunters and those who would destroy his town.

Careful to respect his wishes, we gingerly walked the main street. A handful of crumbling brick and wooden facades stood on either side of us. Most seemed ready to topple if you so much as used harsh language. Yet there was still a hint of dignity in at least a few of these aged dowagers—an elegance in the graceful brick archways over the former doors and windows of the town bank.

Across the way, the collapsed remains of the Cosmopolitan Saloon—which had survived relatively intact until the mid 1980s—testified to the delicate condition of towns like Belmont. The story goes that some local folks were concerned the old two-story Cosmopolitan might someday fall onto a trailer parked on an adjacent parcel. And so one of the most photographed relics of Nevada's mining past was knocked down. In the windows of the front doors, lying askew on a heap of fallen wood, we could see the torn remnants of curtains.

North of the main street was a large, two-story brick building topped with a boxy, 19th-century-style cupola. The Belmont Courthouse—a sign says it was built in 1876 at a cost of $25,000—has survived the ravages of time and vandalism. Standing on a small hill just above the town, the vacant structure still serves to solidly represent the forces of law and order. The courthouse has endured because it was partially restored a few years ago. But, other than the occasional tour by a visiting park ranger, the building is silent until someone can figure out what to do with it.

We circled the ruins in different directions, each shooting photos, entranced by the mood of the place. I thought about the fact that a hundred years ago or so, more than 2,000 people had lived in Belmont. They had left relatively civilized places like San Francisco, Virginia City and Sacramento and voluntarily come to this remote village tucked in the southern end of the Toquima Range. They had struggled through the desert to this place, struggled to find water, struggled to find food and wood, struggled to dig mines and build homes and a town.

After a time, we both started back to the car. There was a cemetery near the entrance to the town we wanted to visit. I turned the car around and started to head west, away from the main street, when the Guardian once again appeared from his trailer and began waving for me to stop.

"Excuse me," he said, sidling up to the car. "Could you please tell me what time it is?"

"Sure, it's about four o'clock," I answered.

He thanked me and began walking back to his trailer. I began to drive away when I spotted him in the rearview mirror, again waving me to stop. I backed the car to where he was standing.

"Excuse me," he said. "Could you tell me what day it is?"

So I told him.

Few mining camps have survived as well and as badly as Austin, Nevada. Located nearly in the geographic center of the state—meaning it's three hours from nearly everything—Austin rivaled Virginia City in affluence and prominence in the mid 19th century.

But the silver ran out—the Spanish have a word, "borrasca," which basically means your mine has crapped out—and the town began to slide into oblivion. A few years ago, Austin appeared on a list of the most endangered historic places in the West. The authors, Randolph Delahanty and E. Andrew McKinney, noted, "Slowly, Austin decays, and with it one of the finest remaining 1860s settlements in the Old West gradually erodes."

Austinites, however, are a feisty bunch and have always been willing to fight for what they want—when they weren't fighting among themselves. A hundred and twenty years ago, when the town needed a church, the congregation passed a hat around and many of the assembled tossed in mining stock certificates. The ample collection was more than enough to build a magnificent church.

A few years ago, when the town's only bank was closed, the folks held a funeral and carried a casket down the main street. When the long-abandoned but still proud St. Augustine's Catholic Church was threatened with collapse because pigeons had nested in the belfry for decades and filled it with tons of guano, a judge sentenced the town drunk, on the occasion of his umpteenth infraction, to shovel out the massive accumulation.

It is only fitting that Austin was also the home of the Sazerac Lying Club, a mythical organization devoted to the art of prevarication—and that the club's very existence was itself a magnificent lie.

*O*VER A CENTURY AGO, THE DISCOVERY OF SILVER MADE AUSTIN NEVADA'S SECOND LARGEST TOWN.

The Sazerac Lying Club was the invention of a bored newspaper editor on a slow day. In 1873, Fred Hart of Austin's *Reese River Reveille* found himself with a blank hole in the paper and no news. Desperate for copy, Hart concocted a story about the formation of a new club, the Sazerac Lying Club, and election of its officers.

While there was an Austin saloon named the Sazerac and its regulars frequently indulged in the blowhard hyperbole created from too many spirits, the club was pure fantasy on Hart's part.

Reaction to the short article was favorable and Hart began to feature additional tall tales, allegedly told at the nightly sessions of the club. Many were picked up by other frontier newspapers, and word of the famous lying club began to spread.

Alas, in 1877 Hart decided to close down the club, writing a humorous final piece about its final session. Shortly after, Hart departed Austin for Virginia City where he worked at the famed Territorial Enterprise (former home of Mark Twain) and, later, in San Francisco.

Austin has always attracted strange characters. One of the town's founding fathers was Reuel Colt Gridley, a grocer and sometime political activist. In 1864, Gridley bet that if his candidate for mayor didn't win, he would carry a 50-pound sack of flour the length of the town, roughly a mile and a quarter uphill.

He lost and, good to his word, lugged the sack up the main street, which was lined with supportive citizens. After his trek, he decided to auction the now-famous sack of flour to the crowd with the proceeds going to the Sanitary Fund, a precursor to the Red Cross.

The winning bidder donated the sack back to Gridley, who auctioned it several more times during the day. By evening, he had raised more than $4,000 in cash (plus several thousand dollars in property deeds) for the fund.

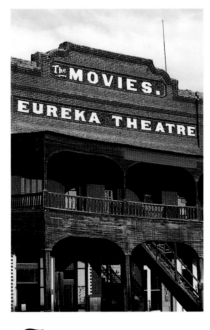

*T*HE EUREKA THEATER

BROUGHT A LOOK AT THE OUT-

SIDE WORLD TO AN ENTERTAIN-

MENT-STARVED COMMUNITY.

The story of Gridley's sack of flour spread and he was invited to conduct similar auctions in other towns throughout the country. During the next year, he would raise between $100,000 and $300,000 (estimates vary) for the Sanitary Fund.

Unfortunately, as a result of his long absences from his store, and the fact his partners had pulled out of the business, when he returned to Austin, he found himself heavily in debt and in ill-health.

He was forced to sell the store and, on the advice of his doctor, moved to California where he died in 1870. Gridley would most likely have been forgotten—he didn't even merit an obituary in Austin's *Reese River Reveille* when he died—if Mark Twain hadn't immortalized the grocer and his sack of flour in "Roughing It."

Today, the famed sack of flour is on display at the Nevada Historical Society in Reno.

Another of Austin's leading citizens was Anson P. Stokes, an eastern investor who had made millions in railroads and mining. In 1896, Stokes decided to build a summer home for his sons who were supervising his holdings in the district. He chose to build the home just south of Austin on a hillside overlooking the vast Reese River Valley.

But Stokes didn't build anything ordinary. He erected a three-story, stone structure, the design of which was based on a medieval tower he'd seen and admired near Rome.

Built of native rock and clay mortar, the tower—which became known as "Stokes Castle"—boasted three floors, each with a fireplace, wooden balconies on the two upper floors, indoor plumbing and a battlemented terrace on the roof.

The castle was inhabited for only a few months in the summer of 1897, then was abandoned. After all, Austin's ghosts needed a place to live.

Just down the road from Austin is the mining

town of Eureka. While never quite as rambunctious as its neighbor, Eureka has its own tales to tell.

For instance, a couple of years ago, the water line in the old Masonic Building burst. A plumber was called and, after turning off the water in the historic 1870s building, he began tapping the pipe through the basement walls to determine the location of the break.

He followed the pipe to the corner of one room, but, to his surprise, there was no door leading into what had to be an adjacent room. Rather, a short hallway led from the first room to the temple chambers, about ten-feet farther, but with no access to the apparent small room in-between.

To fix the pipe, the plumber decided he had to punch through the wall. Once inside, he found a small, square room, the ceiling of which was all the way at the top of the building—like a narrow, two-story empty shaft.

As he stumbled about in the dark, he also felt piles of papers beneath his feet. Perplexed, he collected the papers and brought them out into the light. Upon inspection, he saw they were dozens of letters, packages and newspapers, all with cancelled stamps dating to the 1870s.

*T*HE EUREKA SENTINEL NEWSPAPER BUILDING NOW HOUSES A MUSEUM WITH THE ORIGINAL PRINT SHOP AS IT WAS WHEN IT WAS ABANDONED.

The plumber had inadvertently stumbled onto a treasure-trove of rare 19th-century Eureka mail. Apparently, the upstairs portion of the Masonic Building had once served as the town's post office. Since mining town residents were extremely transient, the Eureka post office had discovered the unusable two-story shaft, which they could access from a slot in the wall, made a perfect "dead letter" file for undeliverable mail. There it sat for more than a century.

An interesting postscript is that in addition to leaky pipes, the aging Masonic Building needed a new roof. The Masons found a Reno stamp collector willing to help them sell their discovery and raise enough money to put a new roof on the building and, presumably, to fix the leak.

Anyone who has ever done business with someone from Virginia City learns about "Comstock Time." Your watch and calendar may tell you one thing, but in Virginia City most everyone is on Comstock Time. This strange, mysterious and wonderous thing allows carpenters to finish their work on time, no matter when it's done, newspapers to be published on time, regardless of how irregular their schedules, and shops to be open during regular business hours, whether that's true or not.

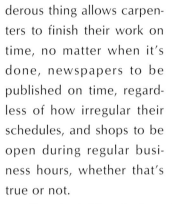

Comstock Time isn't so much a measurement of hours, minutes, or seconds. Rather, it's a state of mind that allows one to accept the notion that the conventional view of time is irrelevant and that things will happen in their own good time.

For years, the best way to measure Comstock Time was to check it by the old Victorian two-faced clock in front of the Virginia City post office on C Street. On one side, the time is accurate. But on the other side, the hands of the clock have been removed.

*G*OOD ADVICE BEFORE DIN-

ING IN A BASQUE RESTAURANT

IS TO SKIP LUNCH.

MEALTIME

"A public establishment masking many private intimacies." William A. Douglass

You can never eat alone at a Basque hotel. One of the unique aspects about dining at one of the dozen or so authentic Basque boarding houses found in Nevada is that the meals are served in an intimate, family style. You sit down at a long table, usually covered with a red and white-checked table cloth, and are proffered food while sitting next to a bunch of strangers. You can find yourself seated adjacent to anyone from a visiting mining engineer to a local insurance salesman.

While not every Basque restaurant operates that way, there are plenty that offer dining in the traditional boarding house manner. The Basque hotel developed in the late 19th century to offer a home away from home for the many Basque sheepherders brought to the American West to supervise the growing flocks of sheep appearing on the open range lands.

The Basques came from an area in southwestern Europe that encompasses the crest of the Pyrenees and includes part of the coast of the Bay of Biscay. This homeland consists of seven provinces that straddle the border of modern day France and Spain. Basques speak a unique language, unrelated to other European tongues, and, it has been said, have never been truly tamed by any monarch or country.

The first Basques arrived in Nevada in the 1890s, during a time when the state's vital mining industry had begun to wane and agriculture was becoming a more important part of the economy. A common myth is that the Basques coming to the West were professional sheepherders or had extensive experience with sheep. Anthropologist William A. Douglass, who has studied Basques in the West, notes that, contrary to that image, most were poor, relatively uneducated and rural. While their rural background provided them with skills in handling livestock, they were generally successful because they were ambitious and worked hard under extremely difficult conditions.

The life of a sheepherder carried with it little social status. In the American West, sheep were considered far less noble than cattle. To be a sheepherder was to be doing something beneath the dignity of most—which made it a job usually reserved for foreign emigrants like Basques.

On the other hand, it was perfect work for a newly-arrived Basque. He didn't need a formal education, didn't have to know English and, if he worked hard, could make enough money in a couple of years to purchase his own sheep and expand his horizons. Within a short time, the sheepherder might be able to bring a relative or friend from his Basque homeland who would repeat the pattern.

The work was demanding and lonely, requiring the sheepherder to spend months in the most remote, isolated, often desolate parts of Nevada, without much companionship. As a result of such conditions, it was almost impossible for most Basques to learn the language and assimilate into American society as did members of most other emigrant groups. Obviously, opportunities for establishing a family were also extremely limited.

Most Basques looked upon their American experience as little more than an opportunity to escape poverty at home, then make enough money to be able to return there to buy a farm or other business (the Basques called these returnees "Amerikanoak"). Because of the attitude that a couple of years in Nevada was a temporary assignment and their difficulties in assimilating, the Basques retained a strong sense of cultural identity.

All of these factors helped create the need for the

Basque hotel. Not every Basque emigrant returned to the Pyrenees. Some sent for wives and family and chose to establish businesses in America, including small hotels and boarding houses. These became the focus of Basque culture in a community. Sheepmen, down from the hills, would flock to the hotels for a warm meal, soft bed and an opportunity to catch up on news from home, read Basque newspapers and speak in their native tongue.

By the beginning of this century, Basque boarding houses had cropped up in a number of Nevada communities, including Winnemucca, Elko, Reno, Ely, Carson City and Gardnerville. Of course, they didn't cater only to Basques but encouraged business from anyone seeking a bed for the night and a good, hot meal.

A few years ago, I decided to have dinner at the Ely Hotel, a small Basque boarding house and restaurant that used to be in the center of the former copper mining town of Ely. I was early and the owner hadn't yet set up for dinner, so I sat at the bar to wait and ordered a Picon punch. Now a Picon punch is powerful drink. A bartender will tell you it's made of some European nut liquor named "Picon" (not related to the pecan, which is a different nut) mixed with grenadine. One Picon punch will make you late for dinner. Two will have you arguing with the bartender about the unification of Europe and, after three, you'll be singing the Basque national anthem while cursing the memory of Franco.

No one has ever walked away hungry from a Basque meal. In addition to seemingly endless courses, the meals include as much of any particular dish that you might want to eat. Specific types and flavors of food may vary, but at most Basque restaurants they'll start you off with a basket of fresh French bread and butter, followed by a tureen of soup, followed by a large bowl of salad, followed by a plate of spaghetti or vermicelli or some other pasta, followed by a bucket of beans, followed by platters of french

A TREE CARVING REVEALS WHERE A LONELY BASQUE SHEPHERD'S MIND WANDERED.

fries, followed by another side dish, usually with vegetables, followed by the main dish, generally a huge slab of marinated and broiled beef or lamb steak. After that feast, some restaurants will bring you sliced apples and cheese and ask if you'd like a bowl of ice cream. At some point in the meal, the waitress or waiter will also bring you a carafe of hearty red wine. Obviously, the secret is to pace yourself.

Sometimes, it's best not to know what you're being fed. Basque cuisine varies as a result of provincial differences (e.g., coastal Basques serve more fish dishes while mountain folks tend toward beef and lamb). Naturally, in Nevada, the Basques have adapted to their surroundings and serve dishes that reflect what's found in the state. The result is a lot of beef, pork and lamb dishes but also rabbit, trout and a subcategory I call "entrail food." The latter includes such delicacies as sweetbreads (animal pancreas), tongue and "mountain oysters" (bull or sheep testes).

Of course, you never know who you will sit next to during one of these Basque culinary overloads. Once, in Ely, I found myself next to three visiting oil engineers who had been testing an area for oil reserves. Their talk of sonic thumpers and other electronic wizardry turned out to be far more interesting than the day-old newspaper (the only kind you can get out there) I'd planned to read.

But I left after they'd finished their third Picon punch and were beginning to sing.

GENOA IS THE OLDEST PER-

MANENT SETTLEMENT IN THE

STATE. NEVADA'S OLDEST

SALOON HOLDS ITS PLACE OF

HONOR IN THE TOWN.

THE GATHERING PLACES

"The cheapest and easiest way to become an influential man and be looked up to by the community at large was to stand behind a bar, wear a cluster-diamond pin, and sell whiskey." Mark Twain

"Our town is so small we take turns being the town drunk." Sign in Austin's Owl Club

Saloons have long been rural Nevada's social clubs, political meeting halls and psychiatry couches. Intimate secrets, heated words, unkeepable promises and tall tales have all been passed at least a time or two over a beer. In most small Nevada towns, the local watering holes are the place where nearly everyone meets, at least some time during the week, to swap gossip, make deals, or just socialize. If a small town is perceived as something organic, then the saloon is its soul. It is where opinions are formed, decisions are made and, occasionally, consensus occurs.

While the alcohol certainly helps loosen tongues and encourage talk, it's not necessary to drink in order to be part of the scene. Indeed, in many cases, small towns don't offer much in the way of entertainment. When there's no movie theater, the satellite dish only seems to be pulling down reruns and you've already seen every tape available at the local video shop, the saloon beckons as a place to visit friends, play a little pool, toss a few coins in a slot machine and be yourself.

Bars don't care if you're rich or poor, highbred or white trash. Sure it helps to have money when you're feeling magnanimous and offering to buy a round for the house—but most small-town bars accept credit if they know you.

And, of course, the small-town politician knows where to find a few votes before every election day, provided his most hardcore constituents are sober enough to find the polling booth on those first Tuesdays. The cagey pols prowl the evening clubs, stopping in at each for an hour or so to renew acquaintances, talk a little zoning, shake a few hands and tell an off-color joke. In some towns, it's not uncommon that a city council will finish up a late night meeting and informally reconvene at a favorite watering hole. Naturally, official business is never discussed, the meeting is properly noticed in conformance with Nevada open meeting laws and the sun is shining at midnight.

Historically, the first business to open in most Nevada mining towns was a saloon. Sometimes, there would be dozens of saloons in a town of a few thousand people—it's estimated that Goldfield had one bar for every 132 people in 1908. Some towns would have saloons, followed by general stores, assay offices, hotels, restaurants and even newspapers, long before they ever built a church. A church was nice to have but a saloon was a necessity of life.

Indeed, only in Nevada would a town take its name from a saloon. In 1908, the Western Pacific Railroad was laying track through eastern Nevada. About 15 miles south of Wells, the railroad erected a construction camp for its workers. According to the story, one of the tents was designated a bar, which a slightly inebriated patron decided to designate with a handmade directional sign. Others came along and misread his crude sign, interpreting it as the name of the camp. Thus, "Tobar" came into being.

Sometimes, even after the ore ran out or the railroad closed down its station, and a town would begin the slow process of becoming a ghost, the saloon would survive. In a half-dozen desiccated towns across the state, like Belmont, Manhattan and Goldfield, you might not be able to find a bank or a laundry—but you can still get a cold one.

The McGill Club in eastern Nevada hasn't changed much over the years. While McGill has gone from a once-thriving copper mining company-owned town to a sleepy bedroom community for nearby Ely, the McGill Club has remained one of the few constants. Other businesses have come and gone—the movie theater has been closed for years, the massive copper smelter was removed a year or two ago and the drug store hasn't been open for a decade—yet the McGill Club has survived.

It's a classic old-style saloon. While the outside isn't much, the interior is dark, mysterious and, yet, inviting. A massive, ornate, mirrored dark wooden backbar—built on the East Coast in the last century and shipped around the Horn in 1907 (those early Nevadans spared no expense in furnishing their saloons)—sits against the south wall, with the barkeep standing between it and a matching long, narrow bar counter. Bottles of various spirits and concoctions line the backbar shelves, giving it the appearance of an apothecary's shop. There is a large jar filled with those unnaturally red, fat hot sausages floating in some kind of cloudy brine and a wire rack filled with bags of beer nuts—the kinds of snacks you never see anywhere but in a bar. A television set with the sound off shows speedboat racing.

The wizened bartender named Norm seems like he's been there forever. He knows everyone who walks in and what they want to drink. Then he jokes he's new in town and hopes the owner lets him stay on—he's only been there 55 years.

The conversation drifts to the new state prison outside of McGill and all the new people it's brought to town. On the one hand, says one man wearing a baseball cap with an indecipherable emblem, it's good because property values are rising and businesses are doing better. But on the other hand, few of the prison jobs seem to have gone to local people, and there's the arrival of the families of the prisoners, most of whom don't have any way to support themselves. He laments that he never had to lock the doors of his house and car until the last year or so.

Sometime later, the bartender asks me if I've seen the "wall" and leads me to a glass display case that covers much of the wall near the entrance of the club. Dozens of black and white photos of smiling young men in uniforms are in the display. He proudly explains that McGill has always been an ethnically diverse town, with many Greeks, Irish, Slavs, Italians and other groups, brought in to work at the smelter. As those groups became assimilated into American life, many of the sons of these immigrants joined the armed services to fight in various wars for their new country. The wall commemorates all the McGill boys, some who never returned, who served in the military.

The mining company recruited these immigrants at places like Ellis Island, with promises of work in McGill. My late grandfather, born in northern Ireland, was one of those who came to McGill to work in the 1920s. So accustomed to the green of the Emerald Isle, I try to imagine what he might have thought when he arrived in dry, dusty eastern Nevada. My answer comes in remembering that he didn't stay long and moved on to Sacramento where he found work with the Southern Pacific Railroad for more than 30 years.

It's amazing the things you think about in a bar.

In Austin, don't be surprised if you run into Elvis in a bar. Located in almost the geographic center of Nevada, Austin is so far from anywhere else that even the TV is a day late. Perhaps because of the relative isolation, Austinites have found other ways to amuse themselves.

"Did you know Bigfoot lives around here?" said one guy, wearing a cowboy hat and sipping on a Budweiser. "And I seen him. Honest."

He looked at me with a mischievous smile and his friend, sitting on the other side of him, nodded vigorously. I took a drink of my beer and looked for help from Butch, the bartender at Austin's International Hotel. He shrugged and began mixing up something called a "fuzzy navel" for a woman sitting at the other end of the bar.

"Sure, and you've probably got UFOs out here, too," I said, recalling that Austin was the home of the legendary Sazarac Lying Club—and thinking these guys were hoping to be charter members of a new chapter.

The guy in the cowboy hat, who was a mechanic, suddenly got serious and related to me that a couple of months ago a man drove into his garage late one night. He said it was pretty obvious the man had risked burning up the engine by driving into Austin, but he figured the guy was worried about getting stuck out in nowhere.

When he asked the man why he'd not parked the car and hitchhiked into town, the man told him that he'd been driving on the road between Austin and Round Mountain when his engine suddenly died. Before he could get out of the car to look under the hood, the sky around him lit up like daylight. He tried to see the source of the light but it was too bright. After a few minutes, the light disappeared and he could start up his car. At this point, he smelled something burning and decided to head back to Austin, which was the nearest town.

"Didn't I see that in a movie?" I said.

The mechanic smirked, nodded and said he was equally skeptical about the man's story until he started to repair the engine. He discovered several parts of the motor were burned or melted, but not as a result of overheating. To this day, he said he has no explanation for the type of damage he found.

The two remained serious after the mechanic finished his story. I wasn't sure whether to believe them. At that moment, a jukebox in the corner, which had been silent until that point, started playing a country song. The weird thing was that no one had gotten up to put money in it.

"That's just the ghost of the International," said Butch. "He does that every half hour or so."

I feebly noted that there must be some kind of timing device on the jukebox to encourage customers to put money in to keep it playing. Butch said, sure that must be it, and winked, but didn't offer to explain.

Maybe the aliens were playing their song.

The late Julia Viani loved her saloon. Nearly every night for more than a quarter-century, Viani worked behind the bar at Joe's Tavern, with her son, Joe, Jr., and other bartenders. Named for Julia's husband who was a longtime state legislator, Joe's Tavern is part watering hole, part museum, part shrine and part junkyard. Until she was in her mid 80s and no longer

physically able, Julia was always available and eager to take visitors on a guided tour of her place.

She liked to start her tour in front of a wall filled with old political signs, browning newspaper clippings and fading black and white photographs. She explained that she and Joe once had a bar in Virginia City before moving to Hawthorne. The rest of the story was on the wall: how her dog, now gone, was once written up in the "Ripley's Believe It or Not! column for longevity; how she was once voted Miss Senior Mineral County; Joe's elections and political friends, including letters from nearly every governor of the past couple of decades; and other things the significance of which only she could explain.

Moving over to the bar, she talked about the various paraphernalia hanging from the back wall, which includes vintage firearms, old golf clubs and a large collection of baseball caps advertising various truck brands and construction firms. Then she led me over to the wall near the bathrooms where she'd hung an antique tin bathtub from the ghost town of Rhyolite, various pieces of farming equipment and one of those classic barroom paintings of a bunch of dogs playing poker. At nearly every object, she asked, "Ain't it beautiful?" before moving on without awaiting a response. One wasn't necessary.

Pull into almost any little town and you'll find them: dark, smoky but friendly places where everyone knows your name. In Eureka or Austin or Battle Mountain, it might be called the "Owl Club," in Genoa simply the "Genoa Bar" (it's also the oldest active saloon in the state, having started in 1866), while in Virginia City it could be the "Bucket of Blood," "The Union Brewery," the "Silver Queen" or the "Delta Saloon."

Ain't they all beautiful?

*T*HE CARONE FAMILY AT
RABBIT CREEK RANCH HERDS
CATTLE TOWARD THE RUBY
MOUNTAINS.

AMERICA'S OUTBACK

"The Great Basin is . . . one hell of a long, dull drive." John Hart

It's hard for people unfamiliar with Nevada to see anything but endless miles of empty, vacant land when they drive across the state. On the interstates, the monotony is broken by the periodic roadside rest areas and the string of small communities that offer up formica-countered diners and truck stops. The interstate system is the pride and bane of America. While you can always count on adequate gas and food (or perhaps that should be in reverse order), there is a sameness to travel on the interstates. The burger in Nebraska is the same as the burger in Arizona. As the world has shrunk, so, seemingly, have the choices.

Fortunately, not all highways and roads are created equal. Out there, beyond the carbon copy interstates, is a vast network of smaller highways and roadways that have somehow resisted the homogenization of travel and maintained at least some semblance of uniqueness and character. While they usually don't offer the conveniences of four or eight lanes or regular rest stops, they do take you through the scenic backroads of America to nearly forgotten communities filled with fascinating and unusual people and places.

In Nevada, this system of smaller highways includes U.S. Highways 50, 95 and 93—roads that transport you through what can best be described as America's Outback.

To truly begin to understand Nevada, you've got to know that the state consists of Las Vegas, the Reno-Lake Tahoe area and the rest. Nevada politicians frequently refer to the latter as "the rurals," probably for lack of a kinder, gentler term. This great mass of territory, which encompasses most of the state's 110,000 square miles, was one of the last regions to be explored in the continental United States and includes about 15 percent of the state's population.

Perhaps because of the dearth of people, there is something strangely appealing about this area. This is the real Nevada. Certainly, this doesn't mean it's where or the way most Nevadans live (numerically speaking, that honor would go to the million people living in the Las Vegas Valley). Rather, it is the place where you will find the essence of what makes Nevada different from Fresno, California, or Bethesda, Maryland.

America's Outback is easy to parody or mock. A few years ago, in *Esquire*, novelist Tom Robbins ventured off the main roads and wrote of his run-ins with the redneck, good ol' boys of rural Nevada who never take off their hats indoors and sit around in bars whining about how "they didn't let us win in Vietnam." He called the state song an "exaggerated belch" and the "chicken-fried steak" the state bird. Perhaps Nevada should feel fortunate he didn't also declare the satellite dish as the official state flower.

But Robbins also admitted to at least some small amount of admiration for the honesty of these real Nevadans. Certainly you're not going to find a lot of fans of Miss Manners in a place like the Owl Club in Austin, but you will find authentic folks. They might mumble over a beer about the "fukenpolitishuns" in Washington and Carson City, or claim taxes are "toogoddamnhigh" (despite the fact that Nevadans are among the lowest taxed people in America). But they're also folks just as likely to lend you a few bucks if you need it to pay the gas bill or offer you a place to sleep if there's no room at the local motel (in the course of my travels, I've been offered everything from the top of a pool table to a child's bunk bed to sleep on).

Rural Nevada is a place where you can be driving on Highway 50—which *Life* magazine once called the "Loneliest Road in America"—and run out of gas 40 miles from Eureka, and have a local drive up, offer to take you back to town (40 miles in the opposite direction from where he was heading), wait for you to get your fuel, and drive you back to your car. Try that in New York City.

A few years ago, a woman from Eureka, California, told me that she and her husband, who was raised in Eureka, Nevada, decided to return to his hometown to visit relatives. They were driving a Mercedes Benz and, after spending the weekend with the in-laws, decided to fill the gas tank before journeying out onto the Loneliest Road. Her husband pumped the gas, paid the attendant, then drove off without replacing the gas cap. They noticed the missing cap in Fallon and, since there are no Mercedes Benz dealers in rural Nevada, wrapped a piece of tinfoil over the opening until they returned home.

About five years passed, and the two decided to once again visit his relatives in Eureka. At the end of the stay, they decided, as before, to fill up the gas tank before returning to California. Her husband noted that the old garage, where he'd fueled up the last time, was closed but another station had opened across the street. After pumping the gas, her husband joked with the attendant that the last time he was in Eureka, he'd left the gas cap off his Mercedes, so he would be more careful this time. The attendant told him to wait a minute, then disappeared into a back room. He returned with a cardboard box filled with hoses, wires, plugs—and a distinctive gas cap for a Mercedes Benz. He explained that when the old station closed, the owner of the new one bought all of its tires and other stock, including this box of junk.

No wonder it's called the Loneliest Road.

Nevada's back highways, linking dozens of the state's small communities, bear vehicles carrying gasoline, groceries, building materials and the other supplies essential to a town's survival. They are the main connection with the outside world, particularly in those communities where the freshest newspapers are usually a day or two old and television reception is downright ugly without a satellite dish.

Of course, it's always been that way. According to historian John Townley, the Nevada portion of

modern U.S. Highway 50, which runs across the state's wide midriff, was originally opened up by George Chorpenning, Jr. in the late 1850s. Chorpenning developed an overland mail route, called the "Jackass Mail" because of his use of mule caravans, and established a series of supply posts between Salt Lake City and Sacramento (with the easternmost Nevada stations established by Howard Egan in 1859).

In 1860, after political and legal maneuvering, the Pony Express assumed control over Chorpenning's stations and started providing mail service from St. Joseph, Missouri, to Sacramento, California, following essentially the same trail. Even later, the Overland Stagecoach and Overland Telegraph line followed the route.

An actual road traversing the wide middle of Nevada was created in 1913 with the development of the Lincoln Highway, the first transcontinental highway spanning America. Originally unpaved, the highway, nonetheless, captured the imagination of the growing number of automobile enthusiasts.

"The Complete Official Road Guide of the Lincoln Highway," published in 1916, notes: "As one speeds over the Lincoln Highway in his modern automobile, it is hard to realize the slow moving oxen, painfully dragging the cumbersome 'prairie schooner' of '49, the women and children riding inside the canvas covered body, the stifling heat, the dust of the desert rising in choking clouds, the attacks by Indians, the want of water and sometimes food and all the suffering and yearning, with the births and deaths which must have occurred in that journey of six or seven months—an almost interminable journey which is made from coast to coast in twenty days with nothing but enjoyment from one end to the other."

Now that's a ringing endorsement.

Paved sections of the road began appearing during the 1920s and 1930s—often paid for by the automobile and tire companies who were eager to persuade people to purchase a car. In fact, you can still find a plaque on the Eureka County Courthouse commemorating General Motors for funding the completion of 22 miles of paved road through that county. Additionally, cities, counties and states began paving roads in an effort to prove they were indeed civilized places to live and do business.

Today, Highway 50 is a two-lane ribbon of asphalt that passes through some of the last open range land in the country. Out here, the cows truly do outnumber the people and the penalties for hitting one with your car are nearly as stiff as for manslaughter. This is the basin and range terrain of the Great Basin. Long, narrow valleys bordered by waves of deceptively high, corrugated mountain ranges. So much sagebrush that if someone ever discovered a useful purpose for the stuff Nevada would become the richest place in the world. Clear, endless skies that city folks can only dream exist. A hundred different species of rabbits, mice, bugs, birds, trees and shrubs that have managed to adapt and multiply in this hard, surprisingly mountainous land. And few people. As newsman Dan Rather once said of Highway 50, "287 miles of no billboards, neon or traffic jams—sounds good to me."

Of course, other roads also span Nevada's Great Basin country, in a north-south direction, such as U.S. Highway 93 and Highway 95. While Highway 50 may be called the "Loneliest Road in America," at least a few sections of Highway 93 along Nevada's eastern spine are more deserving of the designation.

Highway 93 is one of the longest roads in Nevada, stretching some 525 miles, from Jackpot on the Nevada-Idaho border to Hoover Dam, which bridges between Nevada and Arizona. Along the way, it passes through some of the most unspoiled, untamed, undeveloped country in America. After departing from the small gaming mecca of Jackpot (only in Nevada could a town carry such a name) and the high, flat plateau country of southern Idaho, travelers on 93 enter the outer edge of the Great Basin. In the distance to the west is the magnificent Jarbidge Wilderness Area, while about 50 miles to the east is the start of the Great Bonneville Salt Flats.

*W*ELL-WORN CHAPS AND A NEW HARNESS.

South of Wells is one of the more dramatic stretches of the highway. Traveling down the middle of the wide Clover Valley, the road parallels the snow-topped, craggy heights of the east face of the Ruby Mountains and the fertile Ruby Marshlands. At a place like this, you can't help but want to pull off the road, sit on the hood of your car and thank your maker.

Driving down the remote, uncrowded eastern side of the state, the mind can wander, play tricks, conjure images. The hypnotic humming of radial tires on asphalt, the flashing by of an endless supply of yellow center divider lines and the vast landscape, so overwhelming that it never seems to change—all are part of what becomes your driving mantra. Clouds can become the round, open, fat face of a smiling newborn. Or paint ominous shadows on the surrounding mountains, suggesting hidden places with deep secrets. These lonely roads encourage introspection and contemplation. Nevada writer David Toll once described some of the mountains in Nevada "like sleeping women, sprawling languorously across every horizon." Indeed, if you look long and hard enough, you begin to see there is something sensual in the curves and rises of these ranges (of course, when you start to see women in the mountains, that is also probably a good indication that you should take a break from driving).

South of Ely, the highway edges the west side of the Snake Mountains and the Great Basin National Park, which includes Wheeler Peak at 13,063 feet, the highest point completely contained in Nevada (13,145-foot Boundary Peak in the White Mountains of western Nevada-eastern California is the tallest). The 77,109-acre park commemorates the Great Basin region and dramatically illustrates the basin and range terrain. A visitor can, in a relatively short time, go from the sagebrush and cacti of an Upper Sonoran Life Zone, through forests of piñon pine and mountain mahogany, to a frigid Arctic Alpine

Tundra Life Zone, found at above 10,000 feet, which is vividly characterized by the presence of groves of gnarled, seemingly ageless (they can live more than 4,000 years) Bristlecone pines.

Continuing south, Highway 93 passes through old mining towns, like McGill and Ely, where copper was once so plentiful it was used to make doorknobs and rain gutters, and the silver camp of Pioche, rumored to have been such a lawless town that a couple of dozen men were buried in its cemetery before anyone died of natural causes. Other towns, like Panaca and Alamo, grew up providing the fruits and vegetables needed by the mining towns, while Caliente owes its existence to the railroad. Each has plenty of stories, some even true, worth telling and hearing.

But if Highways 93 and 50 can be said to take you through the soul of Nevada, then Highway 95, on the west side of the state, plunges you into its fiery heart. Stretching through the Mohave Desert, bordered by Death Valley, Highway 95 is a wild journey through some of the most rugged and challenging country in the state. This hot, dry terrain is closer to the more common images of Nevada.

Yet even here there is great beauty and diversity. Joshua tree forests, spiky yucca plants, mesquite bushes, greasewood and the always present sagebrush are but a few of thousands of plants and animals that not only survive but thrive in the western Nevada desert. Indeed, this may be the most biologically complicated, fragile place in the West. Species that have managed to evolve to find ways to live here are often the most likely to be damaged by even the most subtle changes in the environment.

For example, there are several endangered species of pupfish, a tiny, nearly transparent pollywog of a fish found in the Amargosa Valley area. Researchers have found that minor changes in water

*N*EVADA'S WILD HORSE POPULATION IS MUCH LARGER THAN THAT OF ANY OTHER STATE IN NORTH AMERICA.

levels and temperature in the natural spring-fed pools where these pupfish reside can affect their limited numbers. Since the water level and temperature are affected by the amount of groundwater pumped in the surrounding valley, it's not surprising that the little pupfish hasn't exactly endeared itself to local ranchers, farmers and would-be developers.

Consistent with much of the rest of Nevada, the quest for minerals greatly aided in the populating of western Nevada. Many of the towns, and former towns, dotting Highway 95 owe their creation to the presence of gold and silver. Tonopah, Goldfield, Goldpoint, Rhyolite and many more that have since been reclaimed by the desert were children of the early 20th-century mining boom in central Nevada. Each of these mining meccas blossomed for a time, made a bid to become the newest Comstock Lode, then fizzled. Some, like Goldfield and Rhyolite, were more spectacular in their failures. Others, like Tonopah, found other ways to survive, including tourism and the military (which has embraced the relative lack of population and remoteness for testing its secret projects and atomic bombs).

Past Tonopah, Highway 95 enters the southwestern edge of the Great Basin. The road travels by Walker Lake near Hawthorne, one of the last vestiges of the basin's unique system of interior drainage. Like Pyramid Lake to the north, Walker is one of those strange, mysterious natural desert reservoirs that seems so out of place because it lacks vegetation. The lake bursts upon your consciousness, perhaps because such a large body of water is so unexpected.

Highway 95 continues north through Fallon, one of the state's main agricultural districts, skirting the edge of the infamous 40-mile Desert, the absolute worst part of the Emigrant Trail across the West.

Horribly dry and nearly barren of vegetation, the 40-mile Desert was the final test of endurance for the early pioneers. The last drop of water and blade of grass were left behind at Big Meadows (now called Lovelock). The next of either wasn't for some forty miles, until the Carson River west of Fallon. Between was an alkali wasteland of soft, sandy soil that slowed travel and, for the many who couldn't or wouldn't continue, became their final stop. Dozens of mid 19th-century emigrant diaries relate the danger and fears of those who encountered the desert and somehow survived its treachery. The trail across the desert was littered with abandoned wagons, dead livestock, furniture, trunks of clothing and other personal items—a veritable 19th-century thrift shop of effects for anyone willing to fetch them.

A SPLIT-RAIL FENCE MAKES A HANDY RESTING PLACE FOR HORSE HARDWARE.

At the stretch of the Carson River that these exhausted, tortured pilgrims reached upon crossing the 40-mile Desert, an enterprising trader set up a post, which became known as Ragtown. The name was derived from the sorry appearance of the emigrants' clothing, which they washed in the river, then hung in the nearby cottonwoods to dry.

On Highway 95, north of Winnemucca, the road parallels the Santa Rosa Mountains and, to the east, Paradise Valley. The latter is an aptly named ranching area that, despite its beauty, has managed to be overlooked in most travel guidebooks. Set in the shadow of the Santa Rosas, a small community, also called Paradise Valley, is a Kodak Moment-Norman Rockwell hamlet with ancient, sagging wooden barns, atmospheric, long-abandoned, wood and brick frontier storefronts, fertile, green meadows dotted with cattle and horses and an occasional farmhouse. You might call it paradise found.

From here, Highway 95 continues its northern march through a tiny roadside stop called Orovada to the town of McDermitt, a former military outpost and Indian school, located on the Nevada-Oregon border.

The long journey on Highway 95, winding from McDermitt to a spot on the Nevada-California border about 75 miles south of Las Vegas, consumes some 600 miles and takes you through a remarkable range of temperatures, climate, topography, altitude and attitudes. In short, if you drive all of Highway 95, you've seen a big part of Nevada—and you probably deserve some kind of medal for stamina.

Nevada's rural highways are America's mythical open road come to life. Something almost spiritual happens when you drive along Highway 50, preferably in a convertible with the top down, music of choice blaring as loud as you can handle, wind blowing through your hair, warm sun baking the top of your head. This is country so uncrowded you can drive on either side of the road (although it's not recommended) because sometimes you won't see traffic in any direction for 50 miles. If you want to stop and lie on your stomach in the middle of the road, you can. If you want to scream out your window, cursing your boss or authority figures in general, you can.

If you want, you can. Sometimes just knowing there is a place where that's still possible is enough.

 DIRT FREEWAY WITH VERY

FEW CARS.

END OF THE ROAD

"Nevada is ten thousand tales of ugliness and beauty" Richard G. Lillard

A couple of years ago, a man named Jack—a fellow Nevada history buff and ghost town hunter—told me a story. He and his wife were driving the dirt roads of eastern Nevada and stumbled upon an abandoned ranch house. On a hill overlooking the house were four graves with small, marble headstones. In a field adjacent to the house was a rusted, old automobile. Jack and his wife wandered about the property, careful not to disturb anything.

As they looked at the ranch house with its peeling paint, broken windows and sagging roof, they wondered about the people who had built it and lived there. Did this house see the birth of children? Was the corral filled with horses and the yard with chickens? What kinds of delicious smells once came from the kitchen? Had the ranch been abandoned because of too many years of bad crops or drought? Or did the family tire of the back-breaking, thankless work?

While studying the old car, Jack noticed that a piece of paper had been carefully folded in quarters and placed inside one of the empty headlight cavities. Jack slowly unfolded the paper, which was brittle from exposure to the elements. On the paper, he found a poem had been carefully written. He handed it to his wife to read. They knew what had happened to the old ranch.

Jack took a notebook from his car and copied the words to the poem, then refolded the paper and returned it to its home in the broken headlight. Later, Jack would share the poem with others.

Pause awhile to breathe a prayer
For the boy who loved this car.
He died that you might walk in freedom
And carry his story far.

He was the oldest son of the hard-working rancher,
He loved his father and mother.
He learned to read in a log cabin school;
He was adored by sisters and brothers.

Heeding the call of his Uncle Sam
To defend his country dear,
And turning his back on college days,
He drove his old Ford here.

Goodbye to mother and sisters,
Shaking hands with Dad,
The rancher's son left all he loved,
Even the old Ford car.

This rancher's son who loved to read
Patted the car as he walked away,
'You sit right here and wait for me;
I'll drive you again someday.'

He fought Hitler's men awhile in France
Then chased the Desert Fox.
He rode in a Jeep that overturned;
They buried him in a box.

Many winding desert roads he'd driven,
Secure in the old Ford car.
But the open Jeep crushed the rancher's son . . .
Another victim of that war.

Back on the ranch his parents mourned
As they buried their younger son.
Mercifully, they didn't yet know
They'd also lost their collegiate one.

After the war, in a flag-draped coffin,
The college boy came home.
They buried him on the western hill;
The old Ford car stood all alone.

Shock and grief take miles to heal.
Seeking comfort by going further,
They sold the ranch and left the car,
Awaiting the older brother.

When the parents died, they returned to their ranch;
They're all on the western hill . . .
Grieving father and stalwart mother
Their younger son and his collegiate brother.

Remember here the rancher's son
Who will never wander far;
For his body lies in the family plot,
Near the rusty old Ford car.

Then I knew what had happened to the old ranch.